A Guide for Using

If You Give a Mouse a Cookie

and

If You Give a Moose a Muffin

in the Classroom

Based on the novel written by
Laura Joffe Numeroff

This guide written by **Deborah Shepherd-Hayes**

Teacher Created Materials, Inc.
6421 Industry Way
Westminster, CA 92683
www.teachercreated.com
©1994 Teacher Created Materials
Reprinted, 2003
Made in U.S.A.
ISBN 1-55734-531-7

Illustrated by
Kathy Bruce

Cover Art by
Keith Vasconcelles

Table of Contents

Introduction and Sample Lessons

Good books can touch the lives of children like good friends. The pictures, words, and characters can inspire young minds as they turn to literary treasures for companionship, recreation, comfort, and guidance. Great care has been taken in selecting the books and unit activities that comprise the primary series of *Literature Units*. Teachers who use this literature unit to supplement their own valuable ideas can plan the activities using one of the following methods.

Sample Lesson Plan

The sample lessons on page 4 provide the teacher with a specific set of lesson plan suggestions. Each of the lessons can take from one to several days to complete and can include all or some of the suggested activities. Refer to the Suggestions for Using the Unit Activities on pages 6–10 for information relating to the unit activities.

A Unit Planner

For the teacher who wishes to tailor the suggestions on pages 6–10 in a format other than that prescribed in the Sample Lesson Plan, a blank unit planner is provided below. On a specific day you may choose the activities you wish to include by writing the activity number or a brief notation about the activity. Space has been provided for reminders, comments, and other pertinent information relating to each day's activities. Reproduce copies of the Unit Planner as needed.

Unit Planner

Date: **Unit Activities**

Notes/Comments:

Date: **Unit Activities**

Notes/Comments:

Date: **Unit Activities**

Notes/Comments:

Sample Lesson Plan

Lesson 1—Mouse

- Introduce the book, using some or all of the unit activities on pages 6–10.
- Read About the Author with your students. (page 5)
- Discuss the new vocabulary with your students. (pages 6–7)
- Prepare for reading the story by completing unit activities on pages 6–7.
- Read the story for enjoyment.

Lesson 2—Mouse

- Read the story a second time.
- Prepare pocket charts and use the Bloom's Taxonomy cards and activities to involve students in critical thinking. (pages 6,7,11)
- Use the Story Summary Sentence Strips on pages 12–13.
- Help students practice vocabulary with Vocabulary Builder. (page 14)

Lesson 3—Mouse

- Retell story, using Sequencing. (page 15)
- Students respond to literature, using Cookie Writing on page 16.
- Assemble the Story-Go-Round on pages 17–18 and, working in pairs, retell story aloud.
- Research mouse-related facts with students, using All About Mice. (page 19)
- Complete Cookie Craze on page 20.

Lesson 4—Moose

- Introduce the book, using some or all of the unit activities on pages 6–10.
- Discuss the new vocabulary with your students. (pages 6–7)
- Prepare for reading the story by completing unit activities on pages 6–7.
- Read the story for enjoyment.

Lesson 5—Moose

- Read the story a second time.
- Prepare pocket charts and use the Bloom's Taxonomy cards and activities to involve students in critical thinking. (pages 6–7, 21)
- Use the Story Summary Sentence Strips on pages 22–23.
- Help students practice vocabulary with Vocabulary Builder. (page 24)

Lesson 6—Moose

- Retell story, using Sequencing. (page 25)
- Students respond to the literature, using Muffin Writing on page 26.
- Construct and write about scenes from *If You Give a Moose a Muffin.* (pages 27–28)
- Introduce (or review) use of contractions. Assist students as needed. (page 29)
- Reinforce vocabulary and vowel usage with Muffin Words. (page 30)

Lesson 7—Both Stories

- Compare and contrast both stories using Alike and Different. (page 31)
- Conduct Cookie-Chip Graph activity and follow-up summary. (pages 32–33)
- Research moose habitats and Alaska. Practice map skills. (page 34) Differentiate story actions by completing Who Did What? activity. (pages 35–36)

Lesson 8—Both Stories

- Learn songs about the mouse and moose. (pages 37–38)
- Conduct baking soda science experiment Bubbling Soda Fountain and follow-up. (pages 39, 40)
- Prepare recipes on page 41. Serve after a puppet show or story time.

Lesson 9—Both Stories

- Assemble the moose and mouse puppets (pages 42–44) and implement by using some or all of the activities on pages 9–10.
- Compose creative writing stories using patterns on pages 45–47 . Share during story time.

Getting to Know the . . .

Books

(If You Give a Mouse a Cookie is published in the USA, Canada, UK & Australia by HarperCollins. If You Give a Moose a Muffin is published in the USA by HarperC Child Books and in Canada, UK, and Australia by HarperCollins.)

Have you ever wondered what would happen if you gave a mouse a cookie? What do you think might happen if you gave a moose a muffin? Two young boys discover what happens in these delightful stories. In *If You Give a Mouse a Cookie,* a boy offers a mouse a cookie. The mouse then asks for a glass of milk to go with his cookie. After the boy gets the milk, the hungry mouse decides that he needs a straw to drink with. Then the traveling mouse asks for a napkin and a mirror to see if he has a milk mustache. After asking for a variety of items, this cookie-loving mouse finally runs the boy ragged, and the story ends with the mouse asking for a cookie again.

In a similar adventure, *If You Give a Moose a Muffin,* a big, hungry moose comes wandering up to another boy's house. The considerate boy offers the moose a muffin to make him feel at home. The moose then asks if he may have some jam to go with his muffin. The boy gives him some jam, but when the moose is finished, he wants more muffins! Since the boy is out of muffin mix, he needs to go to the store. The story continues with the fun-loving moose asking for many things from the boy, and the young host finds himself running this way and that to keep up with the requests. In the end, the moose asks for another muffin from the exhausted—but entertained—boy.

Author

Laura Joffe Numeroff was born in Brooklyn, New York, on July 14, 1953, and graduated with honors from Pratt Institute in 1975. Laura was always an avid reader, and even while growing up she would read as many as six books every week. She also is a talented illustrator, having created the art work for many of her own books. This author enjoys art and music. She is a collector of children's books and calls herself a "film freak." In a recent year, she attended seventy-two movies. Eventually she would like to write screenplays and adult fiction as well as children's books. During the early part of her writing career, Laura held a variety of odd jobs. One such job was operating a merry-go-round, and another was working as a private investigator. Currently Laura Joffe Numeroff lives in Santa Monica, California. She has been quoted as saying that her work is her life and that she hopes to be writing until her last days. We hope so too!

Suggestions for Using the Unit Activities

Use some or all of the following suggestions to introduce students to the books *If You Give a Mouse a Cookie* and *If You Give a Moose a Muffin,* and to extend their appreciation of the books through activities across the curriculum.

Note: Items 1–11 apply to both the stories. The remaining suggestions will use the words "Mouse," "Moose," or "Both" to indicate which activity correlates with which story and in which part of the unit the activity is to be used.

1. Use *If You Give a Mouse A Cookie/If You Give a Moose a Muffin* with other primary and picture books about animals. With both these books, the following themes can be explored:
   - Cause and Effect
   - Consequences of Actions
   - Sequencing of Events

2. Before you begin the unit, prepare the vocabulary cards, story-question cookies and muffins, and sentence strips for the pocket chart activities. (See samples, patterns, and directions on pages 6, 7, 11–13, 16, 21–23, 26, 42–44.)

3. Depending on which story you are working on, use the appropriate suggestions here. Engage prior knowledge and oral language skills by asking the children to identify or recall any cookies or muffins they have recently eaten. Also make a list of what the students know about mice and moose. To create enthusiasm, show pictures of cookies, muffins, moose, and mice.

4. There are several words from both stories that the students will need to be familiar with before you read the stories. By using the overhead projector and projecting the patterns on pages 16 and 26 onto large pieces of butcher paper, make one large cookie shape and one large muffin shape. Write the vocabulary words for each story in the respective shapes. Display these posters so that the students are able to view the words on a continual basis. Notice a sample cookie vocabulary poster here.

If You Give A Mouse a Cookie

probably	napkin
finished	straw
cookie	mirror
mustache	scissors
sweeping	washing
pillow	blanket
comfortable	crayons
refrigerator	drawing
	thirst

Suggestions for Using the Unit Activities *(cont.)*

4. *(cont.)* Following is a sample of a muffin vocabulary poster.

If You Give a Moose a Muffin

muffin	blackberry
eating	sweater
chilly	borrow
buttons	needle
thread	puppets
grandmother	cardboard
scenery	antlers
	clothesline

5. Display the cover of the book you will be reading. Have the children look for any clues that might convey the story's plot. Make predictions.

6. Read the story aloud to discover what happens to the characters!

7. Develop critical thinking skills with the story questions on pages 11 and 21. The questions are based on Bloom's Taxonomy and are provided in each of Bloom's Levels of Learning. Make cookies and muffins (outlines on pages 16 and 26) using these story questions.

8. Refer to the sentences on pages 12-13 and 22-23 to prepare Story Summary Sentence Strips. Cut out the sentence strips. Laminate a set of sentences for use with a pocket chart. Work with students on some or all of the following activities:

    *   In the pocket chart, sequence the sentences in the order in which the events happened in the story.

    *   Use the sentences to retell the story.

    *   Divide the class into small groups and distribute a few sentences to each group. Ask the groups to act out the part of the story represented by the sentence.

    In addition to these activities, you may wish to reproduce the pages and have the students read the sentences aloud to a partner or take them home to read to a parent, sibling, etc.

9. Review key words using the cookie and/or muffin vocabulary pocket chart cards. Pull out the noted words which are highlighted on the Vocabulary Builder, pages 14 and 24. Assist students in completing this activity.

Suggestions for Using the Unit Activities *(cont.)*

10. Read the story aloud again, or review the Story Summary Sentence Strips for comprehension and story order. Instruct students to complete the Sequencing activity on pages 15 and 25.

11. Students can respond to the literature in a variety of ways with the Cookie and Muffin Writing activities on pages 16 and 26. Depending on the written language skills of your students, you could choose one or more ideas from the following list:

    • Reviewing and evaluating the story

    • Summarizing the main idea with supporting details

    • Writing poetry

    • Writing the vocabulary words in alphabetical order

    • Writing about their favorite parts of the story

    • Writing about their experiences with cookies, muffins, mice, etc.

12. After students have completed the Story-Go-Round on pages 17-18, place them in pairs. Using their Story-Go-Rounds, have the children retell the story using the information on their wheels. You may create an effective homework assignment by instructing the students to retell the story to their parents, sibling, etc. (Mouse)

13. Using the books you gathered on mice before beginning the unit, read some interesting facts to the children about these rodents. Assist the students as needed on the All About Mice activity on page 19. (Mouse)

14. Brainstorm with the students different types of cookies. Be sure to list the words on the board or chart paper large enough so that the children will be able to copy them easily. Students will then complete the story frame called "Cookie Craze" on page 20. A tasty touch to this activity would be to bring in several different samples of cookies for the students to munch on as they write. (Mouse)

15. Have the students construct a scene from *If You Give a Moose a Muffin* and write about some of the events in the story. Directions, patterns, and sentence blocks are provided on pages 27-28. (Moose)

16. Throughout both stories, the contractions "he'll" and "he's" are used frequently. This provides a good opportunity to introduce and/or review basic contraction usage and structure. Use the contraction muffins on page 29. (Moose)

17. Introduce or review the vowels with your students. Using the vocabulary muffins, encourage students to identify the vowels. Assist the children with the Muffin Words activity on page 30. (Moose)

8

Suggestions for Using the Unit Activities *(cont.)*

18. Use a Venn diagram to compare the Mouse and the Moose. Have students complete Alike and Different on page 31 by writing in the appropriate areas how the two characters are alike and different. This activity may be presented to the whole class, or you may wish to have the class work in small groups and share their ideas when they are done. (Both)

19. Provide practice in sorting, counting, graphing, and making comparisons by making cookie-chip graphs. Give each child a copy of the graph on page 32 and a resealable plastic bag containing four kinds of the cookie chips: dark chocolate, white chocolate, peanut butter, and butterscotch. Each bag should contain no more than 10 pieces of each kind of chip; provide an assorted number of each cookie chip. Instruct students to sort and graph the cookie chips. Students should keep the cookie chips on their graph work space until they have completed the recording page. Distribute copies of page 33. Have students complete the graphs, record the information, share their results, and then have fun munching the data! (Both)

20. Introduce the map activity on page 34 by giving your students background on the native habits of moose. Use some of the books you collected before beginning this unit. Wild moose inhabit northern forests throughout the world. In Europe they are known as elk and live in Scandinavia and Siberia. They also can be found in the Rocky Mountain states of Utah and Colorado. They live in parts of Maine, Michigan, Minnesota, New Hampshire, and North Dakota. Moose are found all throughout Canada as well. The largest kind of moose, however, lives in Alaska. (Point out Alaska to your students on a map of North America.) These moose stand up to 7.5 feet high (2.3 m) at the shoulder and weigh as much as 1,800 pounds (816 kg).

    Now, sharpen your students' map skills by helping them to locate on the map on page 34 the information needed to answer these questions:
    * What ocean lies north of Alaska?
    * What ocean lies south of Alaska?
    * What country lies east of Alaska?
    * What country almost (but not quite) touches Alaska?
    * What city is almost in the center of the Trans-Alaska Pipeline?
    * What islands separate the Bering Sea from the Pacific Ocean?
    * What is the name of the tallest mountain in North America?
    * What is the name of the capital city of Alaska?

21. Use the Story Summary Sentence Strips to review both stories. Discuss with your students the sequence of events and unique actions of each story. Use the Who Did What activity on pages 35-36. (Both)

22. You may wish to use the Moose and Mouse songs throughout the unit, introducing each song with its respective story. Write the words to the song on chart paper and display in class. Invite the students to invent hand movements to the songs. Use the hand puppets on pages 42-44 to sing along. (Both)

Suggestions for Using the Unit Activities *(cont.)*

23. Demonstrate a chemical reaction of baking soda and vinegar (base and acid) with the Bubbling Soda Fountain activity on pages 39-40. Tell your students that in addition to baking, baking soda has a variety of uses. Because it is a base (the opposite of an acid), when it is dissolved in water it can be drunk as an antacid to counteract acidity in the stomach. Baking soda is made up of very fine particles which in paste form act as a mild abrasive. This paste can be used for brushing teeth. An open box of baking soda in the refrigerator will absorb moisture as well as bad odors in the air; thus, baking soda is also a deodorizer. Because baking soda does not burn, it is a perfect substance to help put out grease fires. Regardless of the age group you teach, be sure to use the term *carbon dioxide* gas with the students and reinforce that what they will witness is a chemical reaction. (Both)

24. Enjoy making some delicious cookies and muffins with your students using the recipes on page 41.

25. For a culminating activity, have your students construct and assemble their very own moose or mouse puppets. Simple paper lunch bags are all that you need. Be sure to reproduce the patterns on card stock or construction paper; otherwise, the moose antlers will need some kind of reinforcement. Use a variety of strategies with these puppets. Some ideas might include these:

    • Sing the songs using the puppets. (Create a moose and mouse chorus.)

    • Act out the story.

    • Students can read aloud their individual writing activities using the puppets. (Cookie and Muffin Writing on pages 16 and 26)

    • Create commercials advertising the book, using the puppets as spokespersons.

26. Another culminating activity involves creative writing. Students create and assemble their own story booklets. The finished product makes for a nice display at Open House and/or Back-to-School Night. See the directions on page 45.

Story Questions

The following questions are based on Bloom's Levels of Learning.

Prepare the cookie patterns as directed on page 16. On each of the cookies, write a different question from the Levels of Learning listed below. Use the cookies with the suggested activities in this part of the unit.

I. **Knowledge** (ability to recall learned information)
   - Name some of the things that the mouse asked for.
   - Why did the mouse want a mirror?
   - Where does the story take place?
   - What did the mouse want done with his picture?
   - How many characters are in the story?

II. **Comprehension** (basic understanding of information)
   - Explain what happened every time the mouse asked for something.
   - Do you think that a glass of milk goes with a cookie? Why?
   - What do you think would have happened if the boy's parents had come home?
   - Can you think of any other stories with mice in them?

III. **Application** (ability to do something new with information)
   - What might have happened if the boy had not given the mouse a glass of milk?
   - What story would you have read to the mouse?
   - Do you think it is all right to keep asking your host for things?
   - Do you think that the mouse will come back again?

IV. **Analysis** (ability to examine the parts of a whole)
   - Why do you think the boy gave the mouse a cookie?
   - Why do you think the mouse stopped at the boy's house?
   - Compare this mouse to another mouse that you have seen.
   - Describe the personality qualities the boy must have had.

V. **Synthesis** (ability to bring together information to make something new)
   - What do you think would have happened next if the story had continued?
   - Would this story have been different if the boy had owned a pet cat? Tell how.

VI. **Evaluation** (ability to form and defend an opinion)
   - Do you think that the boy was a good host to the mouse? What else could he have done to make the mouse feel welcome?
   - Would you recommend this story to a friend? Why or why not?

Story Summary Sentence Strips

The boy gave the mouse a cookie, and the mouse asked for a glass of milk.	
The mouse asked for a straw and a napkin.	
The mouse wanted to look in a mirror.	
The mouse asked for a pair of scissors to trim his hair.	
The mouse asked for a broom to clean up.	

Story Summary Sentence Strips *(cont.)*

The mouse started to take a nap, and the boy read him a story.	
The mouse asked for some paper and crayons.	
The mouse wanted to hang his picture on the refrigerator.	
The mouse became thirsty and asked for a glass of milk.	
And chances are if he asks for a glass of milk, he'll want a cookie to go with it!	

Name _____

Vocabulary Builder

Circle the words that go across (→) and down (↓).

crayons		A P Q F R E L D
drawing		B O U L I T K R
mustache		H M I R R O R A
mirror		C R A Y O N S W
thirsty		T H I R S T Y I
		B G T M S D W N
		I O N C J U I G
		M U S T A C H E

Write the words from the box above in the sentences.

_____

1. Use _____ to draw a picture.

_____

2. The mouse had a milk _____ .

_____

3. A cookie made him _____ .

_____

4. The mouse asked for a _____ .

_____

5. The mouse put his _____ on the refrigerator.

Name _____

Sequencing

Color the pictures at the bottom of the page. Then cut out each square. Paste the pictures in the right order at the top of the page. In the empty box of each picture, write the correct number—1, 2, 3, 4, 5, 6, 7, or 8.

Name _____

Cookie Writing

Name _____

Story-Go-Round

Directions: Color the pictures in circle A. Cut out the circle.

Circle A

Name _____

Story-Go-Round *(cont.)*

Directions: Write your name on circle B. Trace over the story letters with a crayon. Color the entire circle. Cut out the circle and Space #1. Hold circles A and B together with circle B on top. Insert a paper fastener through the center holes. Turn the Story-Go-Round and tell the story as you turn!

If You Give a Mouse a Cookie

Name _____

Space #1

Circle B

Name _____

All About Mice

Read the stories. Decide which answer is the main idea of the story. Circle the best answer.

1. Mice are small animals with soft fur. Mice have round black eyes, rounded ears, and a thin tail. Pet mice are usually white. Wild mice are usually brown.

   a. how mice live   b. what mice look like   c. what mice do

2. Mice have long snouts with many long whiskers on both sides. These whiskers help mice feel their way in the dark. Mice are constantly sniffing their surroundings.

   a. mice eyesight   b. mice friendliness   c. mice whiskers

3. Mice will eat just about anything. Mice especially like grains and seeds. Mice will also eat insects.

   a. mice food   b. mice teeth   c. outdoor insects

4. Wild mice live wherever they can find food and shelter. Any dark, quiet place makes a nice home. Wild mice may build their homes in the corners of garages or in boxes in basements. Pet mice live in cages.

   a. pet cages   b. wild mice homes   c. mice homes

5. The more you handle a pet mouse, the tamer it will become. Soon it will enjoy being picked up. You can even teach mice to do some tricks.

   a. sizes of mice   b. taming mice   c. mice tricks

Name _____

Cookie Craze

Five _____ cookies are in _____

Four _____ cookies are on _____

Three _____ cookies are at _____

Two _____ cookies are around _____

One _____ cookie is by _____

Story Questions

The following questions are based on Bloom's Levels of Learning.

Prepare the muffin patterns as directed on page 26. On each of the muffins, write a different question from the Levels of Learning list below. Use the muffins with the suggested activities in this part of the unit.

I. **Knowledge** (ability to recall learned information)
- Name some of the things that the moose asked for.
- Why did the moose ask for a needle and thread?
- Why did the moose need a sheet?
- Name the characters in this story.

II. **Comprehension** (basic understanding of information)
- What time of year does this story take place? How do you know?
- Is it possible for a moose to talk?
- Why did the moose keep asking for things from the boy?
- What was the boy's mother doing during the story?

III. **Application** (ability to do something new with information)
- Predict what would have happened if the boy had not given the moose any socks.
- Do you think that the boy will tell his friends about the moose?
- How do you think the boy felt about having a moose in his house?
- What would you do if a moose came to your house?

IV. **Analysis** (ability to examine parts of a whole)
- Where do you think the moose lived?
- Why do you think the boy gave a moose a muffin in the first place?
- Compare and contrast this story to *If You Give a Mouse a Cookie.*
- Do you think that the boy and the moose will remain friends?

V. **Synthesis** (ability to bring together information to make something new)
- What do you think would have happened next if the story had continued?
- How would the story have been different if the moose had brought some friends with him to the boy's house?

VI. **Evaluation** (ability to form and defend an opinion)
- What part of the story was the funniest to you? Why?
- Which story did you like better—*If Give You a Mouse a Cookie* or *If You Give a Moose a Muffin?* Why?

Story Summary Sentence Strips

The boy gave the moose a muffin, and the moose asked for some jam to go with it.	
The moose wanted more muffins, so they had to go to the store.	
The moose felt how chilly it was outside and asked to borrow a sweater.	
The moose asked for a needle and thread to fix the button on the sweater.	
The moose asked for some old socks to make sock puppets.	

Story Summary Sentence Strips *(cont.)*

The moose wanted some cardboard and paints to put on a puppet show.	
The moose asked for a sheet to cover up his antlers.	
The moose used the sheet to clean the mess. Then he asked for soap to wash the sheet.	
The moose went outside to hang the sheet up on the clothesline. He saw the blackberry bushes, and they reminded him of the blackberry jam.	
And chances are, if you give him the jam, he'll want a muffin to go with it!	

Name _____

Vocabulary Builder

Circle the words that go across (→) and down (↓).

| muffin |
| sweater |
| antlers |
| needle |
| thread |

M	U	F	F	I	N	K	A
L	S	Y	A	G	B	C	N
S	W	E	A	T	E	R	T
W	I	D	H	Z	F	E	L
N	E	E	D	L	E	A	E
X	I	T	Q	P	J	O	R
K	T	H	R	E	A	D	S

Write the words from the box above in the sentences.

_____

1. The moose wants a _____ to eat.

_____

2. He asks for a _____ to sew.

_____

3. He uses _____ in the needle.

_____

4. The _____ needs a button.

_____

5. The moose has _____ .

Name _____

Sequencing

Color the pictures at the bottom of the page. Then cut out each square. Paste the pictures in the right order at the top of the page. In the empty box of each picture, write the correct number—1, 2, 3, 4, 5, 6, 7, or 8.

Name _____

Muffin Writing

Story Scenes

Directions:

Give each child a large piece of white construction paper or butcher paper.

Have the children draw the house that the boy lived in. Just the exterior outline or some details from the inside are fine.

Reproduce the story blocks and boy and moose patterns on page 28. Color, cut out, and paste the boy and moose to the house.

Using the story blocks, help students use the listed words at the top in sentences that relate the block title to the story. For kindergarten and first grade, writing a single associated word would work. For second and third grades, reinforce the use of capitals, periods, commas in a series, contractions, possessives, etc.

Have the children cut out and glue the sentence blocks to their pictures. It is not necessary to place the sentence blocks in any specific order.

A set of sentence blocks might look like this:

MUFFIN
The moose wanted
jam with his
muffin.

SWEATER
Needle

SOCKS
puppets

SCENERY
They painted the
scenery.

SHEET
The moose cleaned
up with the
sheet.

BLACKBERRY BUSHES
jam

Story Scenes *(cont.)*

MUFFIN

SOCKS

SHEET

BLACKBERRY BUSHES

SWEATER

SCENERY

Name _____

Contractions

Cut out and paste the boxes below on the correct muffins.

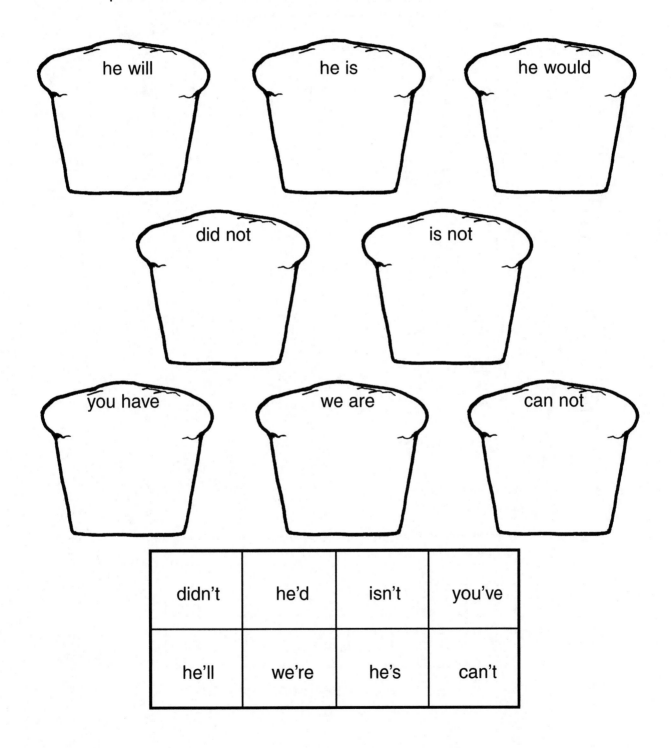

he will	he is	he would
did not	is not	
you have	we are	can not

didn't	he'd	isn't	you've
he'll	we're	he's	can't

Name _____

Muffin Words

Directions: Cut and paste the missing vowel letters for the words in the muffin.

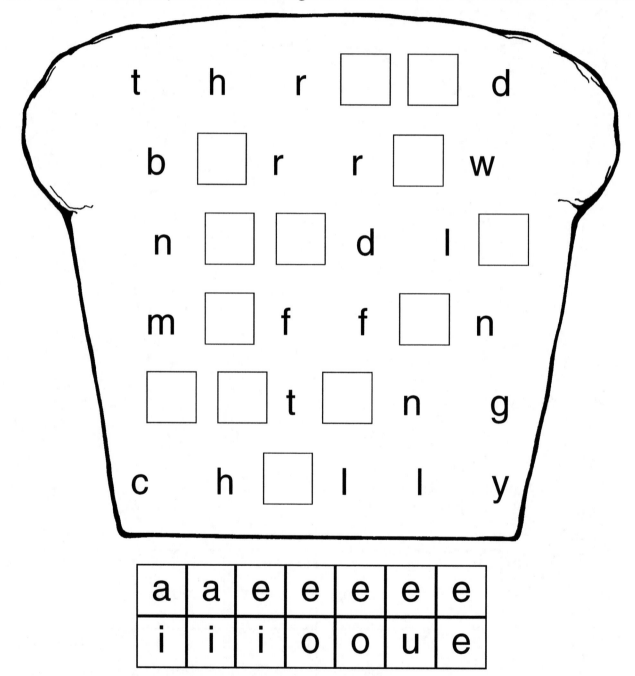

t h r □ □ d

b □ r r □ w

n □ □ d l □

m □ f f □ n

□ □ t □ n g

c h □ l l y

a	a	e	e	e	e	e
i	i	i	o	o	u	e

Word Bank: muffin, eating, borrow, chilly, thread, needle

Name _____

Alike and Different

Directions: In the muffin and cookie, write your ideas or draw pictures of how the two stories are alike and different. Show likenesses in the middle where the cookie and muffin overlap.

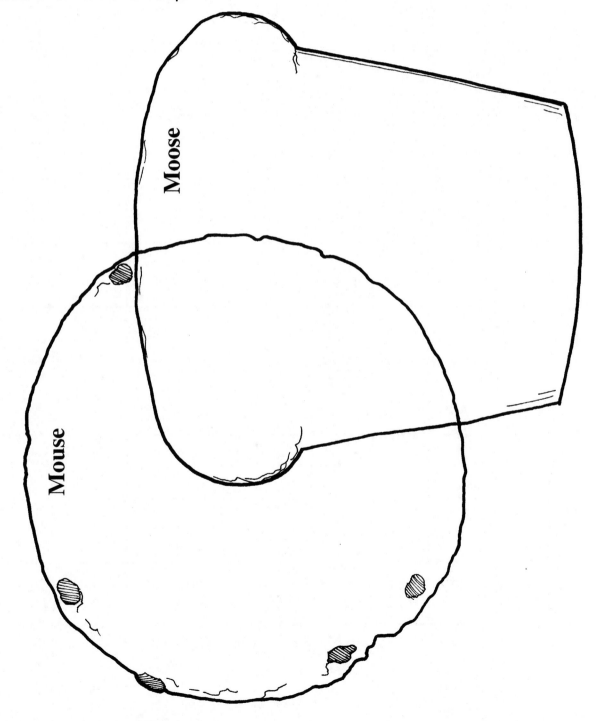

Moose

Mouse

Name _____

Cookie-Chip Graph

	Dark Chocolate Chips	Butterscotch Chips	White Chocolate Chips	Peanut Butter Chips
10				
9				
8				
7				
6				
5				
4				
3				
2				
1				
0				

KINDS OF COOKIE CHIPS

Name _____

Cookie-Chip Graph Recording Sheet

Directions: Use the information from your graph to fill in the blanks below.

Recording Information

My cookie-chip graph has . . .

_____ dark chocolate chips

_____ butterscotch chips

_____ white chocolate chips

_____ peanut butter chips

Graph Summary

I made these discoveries:

My graph has more _____

    than any other kind of cookie chip.

My graph has fewer _____

    than any other kind of cookie chip.

My friend's graph has more _____

    than any other kind of cookie chip.

My friend's graph has fewer _____

    than any other kind of cookie chip.

I like to eat _____

    more than any other kind of cookie chip.

Name _____

Alaska—The Moose's Home

Directions: Use the map on this page to answer your teacher's questions. When you are finished, you may color this map of Alaska.

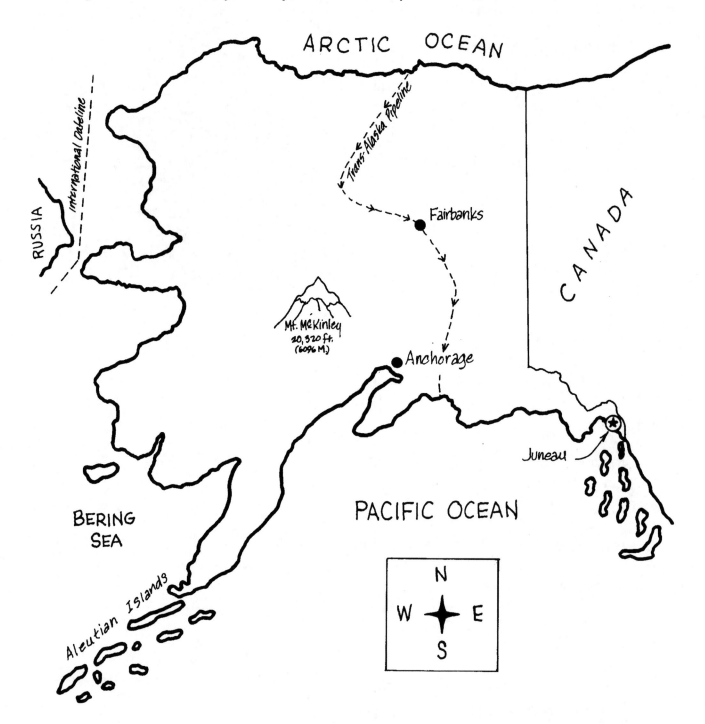

Name _____

Who Did What?

Directions: Read each of the boxes. Decide if the mouse or the moose did what is in each box. Cut out all of the moose and mouse boxes on page 36. Paste a mouse or mouse in the correct square.

Who asked for a straw?	Who wanted some jam?	Who asked for some soap?
Who made some puppets?	Who asked to borrow a sweater?	Who asked for a story?
Who asked for a sheet?	Who asked for a broom?	Who asked for some scissors?
Who asked for a pen?	Who asked for some crayons?	Who asked for a needle and thread?

Who Did What? *(cont.)*

Directions: Color and cut out the moose and mouse boxes.

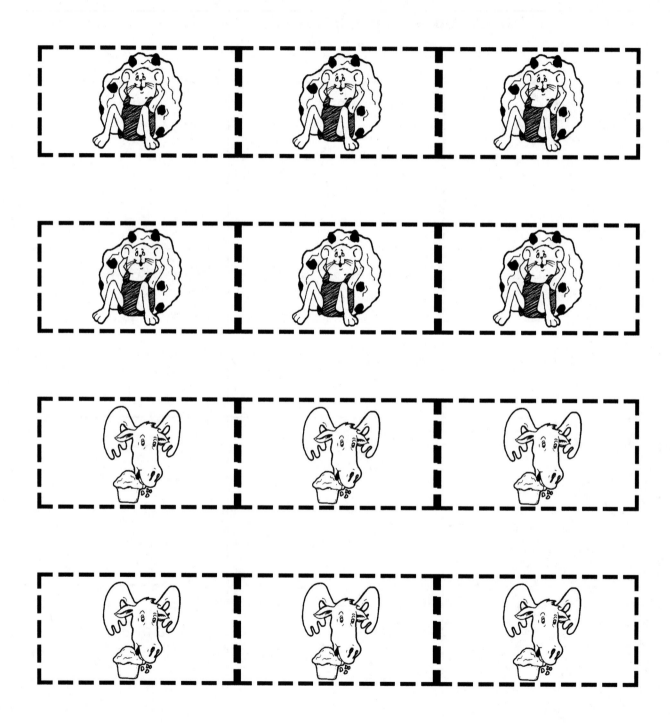

Mouse Sing-Along Song

Sing to the tune of "Three Blind Mice."

If you give a mouse a cookie,
If you give a mouse a cookie,
He'll want a glass of milk,
He'll want a glass of milk,
He'll ask for a straw and a napkin too,
He'll look in the mirror and wonder who,
He'll ask and ask and ask of you,
If you give a mouse a cookie.

If you give a mouse some scissors,
If you give a mouse some scissors,
He'll give himself a trim,
He'll give himself a trim,
He'll ask for a broom and sweep and sweep,
He'll clean your house and make it neat,
He'll ask and ask and ask of you,
If you give a mouse some scissors.

If you give a mouse a blanket,
If you give a mouse a blanket,
He'll want a pillow too,
He'll want a pillow too,
He'll want a story read to him,
He'll look at the pictures again and again,
He'll ask and ask and ask of you,
If you give a mouse a blanket.

If you give a mouse a crayon,
If you give a mouse a crayon,
A picture he will draw,
A picture he will draw,
He'll sign his name with a pen,
Tape it on the fridge and then,
He'll ask and ask and ask of you,
If you give a mouse a crayon.
(Repeat the first verse.)

Moose Sing-Along Song

Sing to the tune of "She'll Be Coming Around the Mountain"
or "If You're Happy and You Know it, Clap Your Hands."

If you give a moose a muffin, he'll want more;
If you give a moose a muffin, he'll want more;
If you give a moose a muffin,
He'll want jam for the stuffin';
If you give a moose a muffin, he'll want more.

If you give a moose some jam, he'll want more;
If you give a moose some jam, he'll want more;
If you give a moose some jam,
He will eat all that he can;
If you give a moose some jam, he'll want more.

If you give a moose a sweater, he'll want more;
If you give a moose a sweater, he'll want more;
If you give a moose a sweater,
He will want to make it better;
If you give a moose a sweater, he'll want more.

If you give a moose a button, he'll want more;
If you give a moose a button, he'll want more;
If you give a moose a button,
He'll want socks to make a puppet;
If you give a moose a button, he'll want more.

If you give a moose some socks, he'll want more;
If you give a moose some socks, he'll want more;
If you give a moose some socks,
He'll play puppets in a box;
If you give a moose some socks, he'll want more.

If you give a moose a sheet, he'll want more;
If you give a moose a sheet, he'll want more;
If you give a moose a sheet,
A scary ghost he'll want to be;
If you give a moose a sheet, he'll want more.
(Repeat the first verse.)

Bubbling Soda Fountain

In Laura Joffe Numeroff's stories, the cookie and muffin served as starting points for fun, havoc, and adventures. In some cookies and muffins (as well as many other baked goods) an important ingredient is baking soda. Here is an opportunity to "wow" your students by using baking soda in a fashion other than cooking to create a bubbling "soda fountain"!

Materials:

- baking soda
- water
- liquid detergent (or soap powder)
- vinegar
- a tall bottle (Old-fashioned soda bottles are perfect.)

Procedure:

1. Show your students the box of baking soda. Explain that it is an important ingredient in cookies and muffins because it helps the dough to rise and become lighter. Tell your students that they will be observing a chemical reaction using baking soda.

2. Pour 2 cups (500 mL) of water into the tall bottle. Add 1 tablespoon (15 mL) of baking soda and a few drops of liquid detergent or a pinch of soap powder. Let this mixture dissolve.

3. Observe the bottled mixture with your students. Tell the students that you will be adding some vinegar next. Make predictions about what might happen to the mixture.

4. Pour in a few tablespoons of vinegar. The chemical reaction produces tiny soap bubbles filled with carbon dioxide gas. The foam rises up and flows over the top of the bottle in a fountain of bubbles. Explain to your students that by mixing all of these ingredients, carbon dioxide gas is formed.

Science Facts:

Baking soda that is dissolved in water will react with acids (like vinegar or sour milk) to produce carbon dioxide gas. In cooking, the gas bubbles in the dough make the final baked goods lighter in texture. An additional activity to go along with the baking section of this book would be to prepare some cookie dough without baking soda. (Or a small portion of cookie dough could be set aside before adding the baking soda.) Bake both batches of dough and compare the differences in the final products.

Name: _____

Bubbling Soda Fountain *(cont.)*

Write the ingredients that your teacher used.

1. _____   2. _____

3. _____   4. _____

What did all the ingredients form? _____

Draw a picture of what happened.

Muffins and Cookies

The following is a recipe for old-fashioned muffins. This recipe will yield one dozen muffins.
For variety, add some blueberries, cranberries, or applesauce to the recipe.

Moose Muffins

2 cups (500 mL) all-purpose flour
2 tablespoons (30 mL)sugar
1 tablespoon (15 mL) double-acting baking powder
¹/₂ teaspoon (2.5 mL) salt
1 egg
1 cup (250 mL) of milk
¹/₄ cup (63 mL) of salad oil

Preheat the oven to 400 F (204 C). With butter or a non-stick spray, grease the muffin-pan
cups. Using a large bowl, mix the flour, sugar, baking soda and salt together. In a small
bowl, beat the egg, and then gradually add the milk and salad oil. Add this mixture to the
large bowl and stir briefly with a wooden spoon until the flour is just moistened. Spoon the
batter into the greased muffin-pan cups, filling each about 2/3 full. Bake the muffins for 20 to
25 minutes until they are golden brown. Serve warm and don't forget the jam!

Mouse Style Cookies

The following recipe will yield about four dozen cookies.

1³/₄ cups (438 mL) all-purpose flour
¹/₂ cup (125 mL) packed light brown sugar
¹/₂ cup (125 mL) of white sugar
¹/₂ cup (125 mL) butter, softened
1 egg
1 teaspoon (5 mL) vanilla extract
¹/₂ teaspoon (2.5 mL) baking soda
¹/₂ teaspoon (2.5 mL) salt
16 ounce (450 g) package of chocolate chip pieces
¹/₂ cup (125 mL) walnuts, optional

Preheat the oven to 375°F (190°C). With butter or a non-stick spray, grease four cookie
sheets. Into a large bowl, measure all the ingredients except for the chocolate chip pieces.
With a mixer at medium speed, beat until well mixed. Add in the chocolate chip pieces and stir
well. Drop by rounded teaspoonfuls, 2 inches (5 cm) apart, on the cookie sheets. Bake for
10-12 minutes, or until the cookies are lightly browned. Serve warm and don't forget the milk!

Puppet Patterns

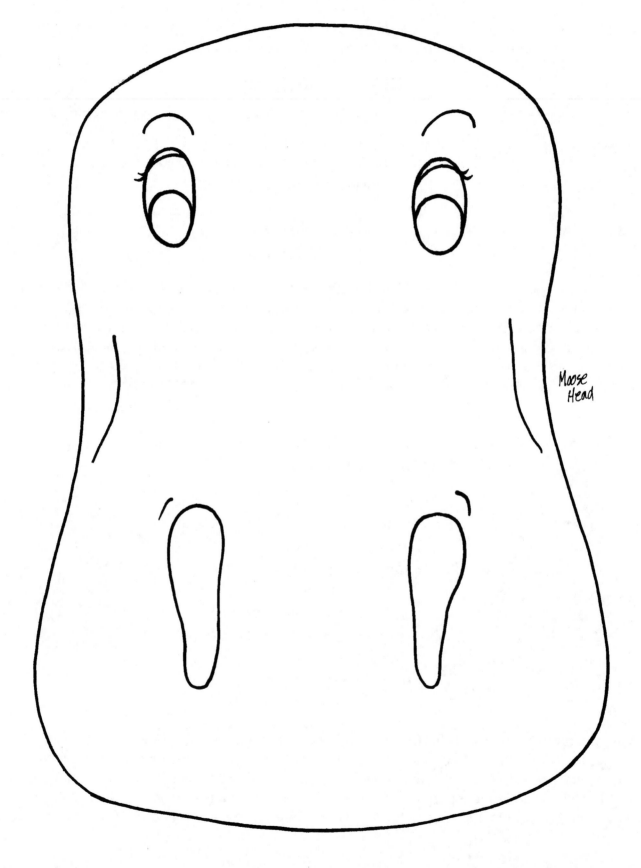

Moose
Head

Puppet Patterns *(cont.)*

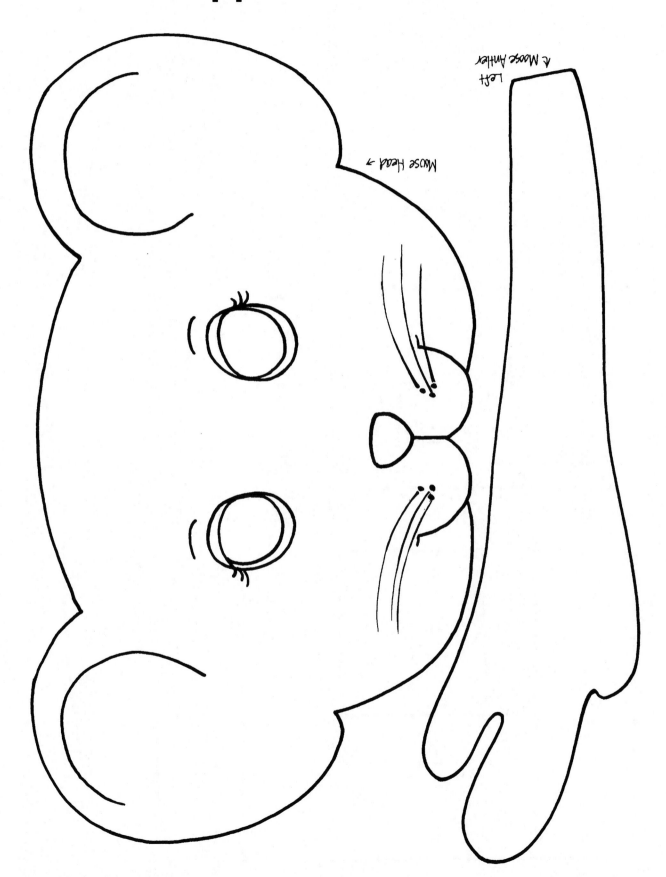

Moose Head →

Left & Moose Antler

Puppet Patterns *(cont.)*

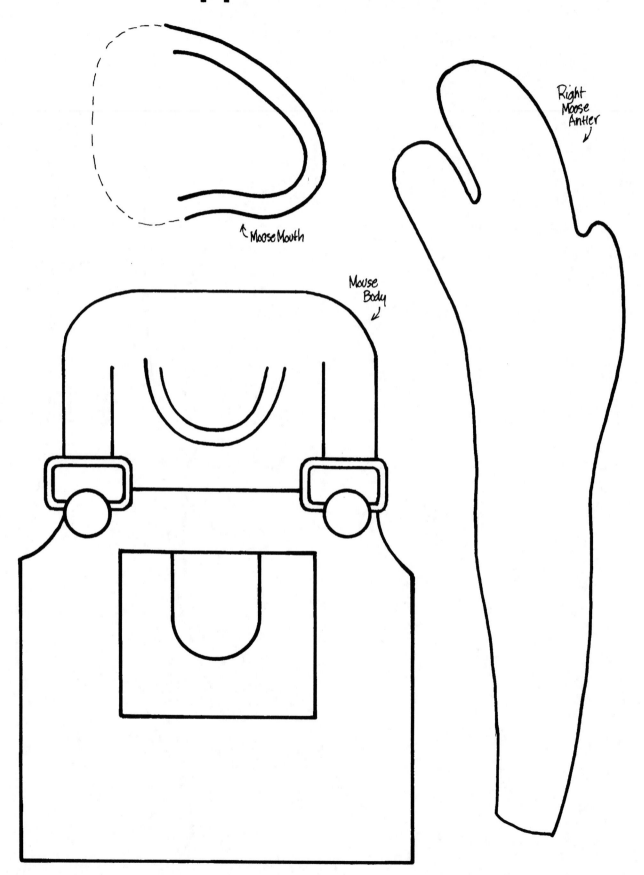

Moose Mouth

Right Moose Antler

Mouse Body

Story Booklets

As a culminating activity for this unit, invite your students to use their imaginations and create their own versions of the moose and mouse stories. Or challenge the children to invent their own related story. For students writing their own, possible options would be these:

- If You Give a Dog a Bone
- If You Give a Rabbit a Carrot
- If You Give an Elephant a Peanut
- If You Give a Monkey a Banana

Depending on which story line your students choose, reproduce the appropriate story frames. For students writing their own versions of Laura Numeroff's stories, use the cookie pattern on page 16 and the muffin pattern on page 26. Choose the best age-appropriate number of pages for the students' books. Reproduce enough patterns to include a cover. Staple the patterns together to form a booklet. After an initial draft has been completed, edited, and revised, students then will copy their stories on the final booklet paper.

Encourage students to share their stories with the rest of the class. Visit another class and give your students the opportunity to do some storytelling in front of a larger audience. Display the finished stories on your story bulletin board.

Some possible stories might look like this:

If You
Give a Dog
a Bone
by Kristin

If you walk
him, he'll chase
a cat.

If you give a dog
a bone, he'll want
to be petted.

If he chases
a cat, he'll start
barking. So pet him.

If you pet him,
he'll want to go
for a walk.

But if you
pet him,
he'll want another bone!

Story Patterns

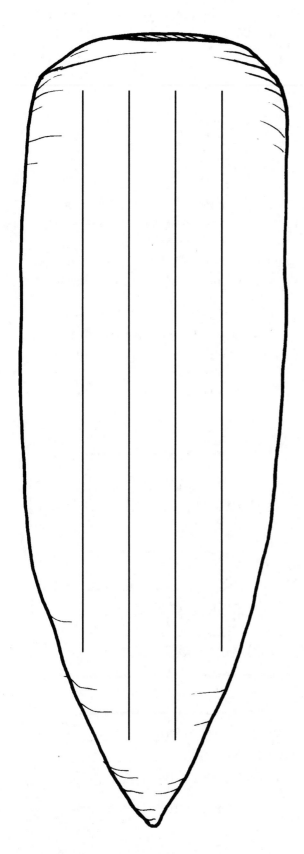

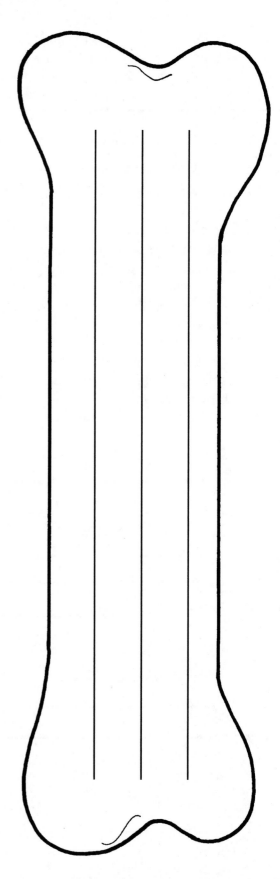

Story Patterns *(cont.)*

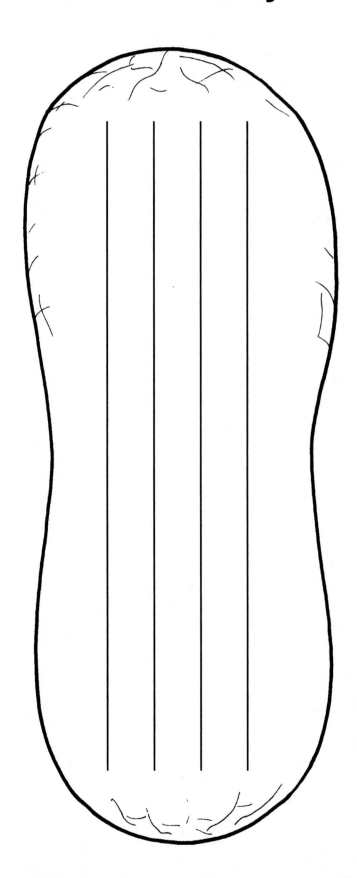

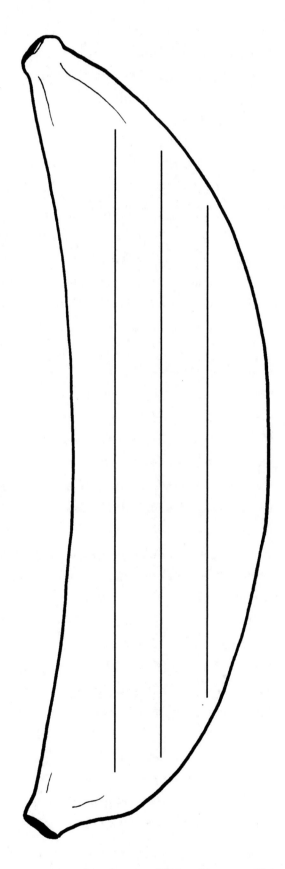

Bibliography

Other Books by Laura Joffe Numeroff

Amy for Short. Macmillan, 1976.

Beatrice Doesn't Want to. F. Watts, 1981.

Does Grandma Have an Elmo Elephant Jungle Kit? Greenwillow, 1980.

Emily's Bunch. Macmillan, 1978.

The Ugliest Sweater. F. Watts, 1983.

Walter. Macmillan, 1978.

You Can't Put Braces on Spaces. Greenwillow, 1979.

Related Literature

Abolafia, Yossi. *A Fish for Mrs. Gardenia.* Greenwillow, 1988.

Asch, Frank, and Vladimir Vagin. *Here Comes the Cat!* Scholastic, 1989.

Aurego, Jose. *Look What I Can Do.* Macmillan Child Grp., 1988.

Bancroft, Catherine, and Hannah C. Gruenberg. *Felix's Hat.* Macmillan, 1993.

Barret, Judi. *Animals Should Definitely Not Act Like People.* Macmillan Child Grp., 1988.

Bernier, Evariste. *Baxter Bear and Moses Moose.* Down East, 1990.

Blacker, Terence. *Herbie Hamster.* Random, 1990.

Bourgeois, Paulette. *Too Many Chickens!* Little, 1991.

Brown, Marc. *Arthur Meets the President.* Little, 1991.

Calhoun, Mary. *High Wire Henry.* Morrow, 1991.

Corey, Dorothy. *Everybody Takes Turns.* A. Whitman, 1980.

Donaldson, Julia. *A Squash and a Squeeze.* Macmillan, 1993.

Dr. Seuss. *Thidwick, the Big-Hearted Moose.* Random Bks Yng Read., 1948.

Evans, Nate. *The Mixed-Up Zoo of Professor Yahoo.* Jr. League, 1993.

Forest, Heather. *The Baker's Dozen.* HarBrace J., 1988.

Greene, Carol. *The Insignificant Elephant.* Harcourt, 1985.

Gwynne, Fred. *Pondlarker.* Simon & Schuster, 1990.

Hutchins, Pat. *The Doorbell Rang.* Morrow, 1989.

Johnston, Tony. *Mole and Troll Trim the Tree.* Dell, 1989.

Littledale, Freya. *The Farmer in the Soup.* Scholastic, Inc., 1987.

Luttrell, Ida. *Mattie's Little Possum Pet.* Macmillan, 1993.

Mayer, Mercer. *What Do You Do with a Kangaroo?* Scholastic, 1987.

McAllister, Angela. *Matepo.* Dial, 1991.

Ochs, Carol. *Moose on the Loose.* Down East, 1987.

Reese, Bob. *Mickey Mouse.* ARO, 1986.

Ross, Tony. *I Want a Cat.* Farrar, 1989.

Wickstrom, Sylvie. *Turkey on the Loose.* Dial, 1990.

Worthington, Phoebe. *Teddy Bear Baker.* Penguin, 1989.